AN AMAZING ADVENTURE

The Story of a Grey Seal Pup

To Barbara

Best wishes,

Ken Crossan

AN AMAZING ADVENTURE

The Story of a Grey Seal Pup

Written and Photographed by Ken Crossan

Fireflash Publishing 2016

ISBN: 978-0-9934765-2-5

Published by Fireflash Publishing

Printed and bound by Blissetts, London

PREFACE

With its soft, creamy-white fur and large, dark, engaging eyes, the pup of the grey seal is one of the most endearing creatures in the animal kingdom. Over one-third of the world's grey seals are born around Scotland's mainland coastline and islands.

Although pupping beaches tend to be remote and free from disturbance, I am fortunate to have an accessible beach close to my home in Caithness in the far north of Scotland. This beach has relatively few pups and, as the pup whose growth and behaviour I was to follow tended to stay away from the other seals, I was able to establish a unique photographic record without disturbance to the rest of the colony.

I went to the beach at the same time each day, wearing the same clothes (or, at least, the same outer clothing) and, lying on the beach each day, I realised quite quickly that I began to smell like a seal! As I was around regularly each day from shortly after the time of its birth, the pup accepted me as part of its environment, behaved quite naturally throughout and never displayed any signs of stress or distress in my presence.

In many years of observing grey seals, I have rarely witnessed the behaviours displayed by this seal pup. It was very active and inquisitive from the outset, exploring the beach extensively yet keeping its distance from the other seals. Moreover, it tested out the water from an early age and spent much more time in the water both before and after its moult than would have been expected.

I invite you to join with me and celebrate yet another wonder of nature as we follow the adventures of the grey seal pup from a helpless newborn to an independent juvenile prepared to face the challenges of entering the North Sea.

Ken Crossan

DAY 1a

I am a grey seal pup and my amazing adventure begins on the 2nd November when I was born on a beach in Caithness in the far north of Scotland.

I am a healthy pup. I am almost a metre long and I weigh around 14 kilogrammes.

Amazing Factfile

The grey seal is Britain's biggest mammal and largest carnivore. A mature adult male may reach 2.5 to 3.3 metres long and weigh up to 300 kilogrammes, whereas the smaller female can grow to between 1.6 and 2 metres in length and weigh between 100 and 150 kilogrammes.

DAY 1b

As soon as I was born, mum turned round immediately to sniff me and to call to me. This allowed us to bond, learning each other's smell and voices within a few minutes of my birth. This means that my mum will be able to recognise me amongst other seal pups on the beach.

You can see that my umbilical cord is wrapped around my body and is still attached to the placenta, or afterbirth. However, the umbilical cord snapped and the placenta broke away as soon as I left this flat rock on which I was born.

Amazing Factfile

The grey seal is the more common of Britain's two species of seal (the other being the common, or harbour, seal). It is reckoned that around 40% of the world's grey seals live in the waters around the UK. The current UK population is estimated at approximately 112,000 of which 90% breed in Scotland.

DAY 2

It's amazing how quickly Mother Nature has cleaned me up! The rocks on which I was born and in which I sheltered on the day of my birth can be seen in the distance. However, rather than just resting up amongst these rocks like the other pups, I am already behaving quite differently and my adventurous nature has led me to explore the beach away from the rest of the colony.

It's been tiring hauling myself around at such a young age so it's time for a sleep to rest and conserve my energy.

Amazing Factfile

Grey seals are separated into three distinct populations – the western Atlantic population is centred in the Canadian Maritime provinces, whilst the eastern Atlantic population is found mostly around the coasts of the United Kingdom and Ireland, as well as on the coasts of the Faroe Islands, Iceland, Norway and northwestern Russia. The third population is located in the Baltic Sea.

DAY 3

Today I've continued my amazing adventure by exploring more of the beach. This area of the beach is quite empty and, as few other seal pups are born here, I have plenty of space to roam around.

Traditional grey seal pupping sites like my beach are called 'rookeries'. Individual adult females, or cows, will visit this site every year for mating and pupping.

Amazing Factfile

Grey seals establish rookeries in a variety of habitats where disturbance is minimal. Breeding territories are to be found on rocky islands and coasts, in caves, sandy islands and beaches. In more severe climes, grey seals breed on ice floes or pack ice.

DAY 4a

I've done quite a bit more exploring of the beach today and I'm now having a well-earned sleep. Lying like this, you can see my umbilical cord and this will wither and fall off within the next few days.

Mum tends to remain just offshore while I am on the beach and she is keeping an eye on me from the water's edge to make sure that I am safe.

Amazing Factfile

The thick, creamy-white fur of the grey seal pup is known as the 'lanugo'. This is also the term that is used for the very fine, soft, downy hair that covers a newborn baby. Lanugo is the Latin word for 'down'.

DAY 4b

I've woken up thirsty and, as ever, mum is there ready to feed me when I call.

Although she always only has one pup, mum has two teats and I switch from one to the other every few seconds so that I can get as much milk as possible.

I suckle from mum five or six times a day, for up to ten minutes at a time.

Amazing Factfile

The mother's milk contains up to 60% fat, so pups grow very quickly, gaining up to 2 kilogrammes in weight each day. The weight gain consists mainly of a layer of blubber below their skin, which is vital insulation when they are ready to go to sea.

DAY 5

It's time for a play where I can stretch, yawn and even have a little nibble of my front flippers, although I have to be a little careful of the claws.

I have a fine set of teeth, even at this age, and these will grow as I grow.

Amazing Factfile

The deciduous teeth of the grey seal shed before birth. It is possible to age seals quite accurately by counting the growth rings round the roots of the back teeth.

DAY 6a

It's a big day today in my amazing adventure. Although most pups do not venture into the water for their first three or four weeks, I am again going to be adventurous.   The temptation of the water is too great and, even though I am only six days old, the bay seems quite calm so I have decide to go into the shallow waters to see what it's like.

Amazing Factfile

Most pups rarely go into the sea for the first three weeks or so of their lives because they are not very proficient at swimming and because their soft, white fur is not waterproof and they are, therefore, at risk of being swept out to sea and drowning.

DAY 6b

Although I stayed in the shallows of the water's edge, the waves caught me, dragged me out into the bay then tossed me back towards the shore. I have decided to stay around the rocks for a bit of protection.

Amazing Factfile

The mortality rate for pups is around 15%, but can be as high as 30-55% in their first year. Pups can be crushed during the breeding season, particularly in colonies of high population densities, or be washed out to sea during severe storms.

DAY 6c

Mum spotted me being tossed about in the water and came over to keep an eye on me and to make sure that I was safe and not too adventurous.

Amazing Factfile

Grey seals are also very sensitive to any disturbance at their breeding sites which can result in females losing their maternal bond with their pups leading to abandonment.

DAY 6d

I'm so pleased that mum came over to me to make sure that I stayed safe. It has given me a chance to play with her and cuddle up to her in the water.

Amazing Factfile

If they survive the dangers of being a pup, grey seals are relatively long-lived - bulls around 25 years and cows around 35 years, although one female in the Shetland Islands was known to be 46 years old.

DAY 7

After all the excitement of playing in the water yesterday, I thought it best to have a restful day on the beach today.

Amazing Factfile

Female grey seals reach sexual maturity at between three and five years old and may become pregnant and give birth to a pup a year later.

DAY 8a

I can't resist it. I'm back into the breaking waves on the shoreline today to explore the calmer waters around the rocks and play with mum again.

Amazing Factfile

On the other hand, male grey seals reach sexual maturity at between four and six years old but may not attain territorial status until eight to ten years of age.

DAY 8b

It's been exhausting playing in the water. It's time for a big snooze amongst the rocks on the shore.

Amazing Factfile

Since many seals die at sea, it is difficult to know the major causes of death. Diseases caused by parasites, pollution (either in the form of toxins or oil) and drowning in fishing nets are some of the main reasons.

DAY 9

I've been exploring the beach again today, as well as playing in the water. I've just had a feed and I'm having a rest amongst the rocks with mum keeping an eye on me from the shoreline. I'll soon be ready to put my head down and have an afternoon sleep.

Amazing Factfile

The name 'grey' seal is rather misleading since there is a high degree of colour variation amongst individuals. Male and female grey seals differ in colour: males are dark grey, brown and black with some lighter blotches over the fur, whilst females are generally light grey with darker blotches. After the pup has moulted, the coat pattern shown by the juvenile seal reflects these sex differences.

DAY 10

Because I love playing in the water so much, mum will quite often encourage me to come in and join her. My swimming skills are improving although it is still quite a challenge because my white fur is not waterproof and gets quite soggy.

Amazing Factfile

In addition to coat markings, the nose of the grey seal can distinguish male from female. The male grey seal has a long, arched Roman nose which is the basis for its Latin name, Halichoerus gryptus, meaning 'the hook-nosed sea pig'.

DAY 11

I'm still staying away from the other seals on the beach which is giving me lots of room to explore. I can also have peace and quiet to lie on my back and just chill out.

Amazing Factfile

> Grey seals feed on a wide variety of open-sea and bottom-dwelling fish, although sandeels and cod are their most important foods. The daily food requirement of the adult is about 5 kilogrammes, although adult seals do not feed every day.

DAY 12

I'm in the bay again today playing with mum in deeper parts away from the water's edge. We both enjoy the interaction and contact and mum doesn't even seem to mind when I hitch a piggy-back ride on her back!

Amazing Factfile

Grey seals are, however, opportunistic feeders and will eat whatever is available, including octopus and lobsters. They can also be found swimming between fishing boats in harbours to take advantage of discarded catch.

DAY 13a

It really is great fun playing with mum in the deeper waters. Mum is very patient with me and doesn't seem to mind me snuggling in to her neck.

Amazing Factfile

When feeding, small fish are taken whole, while the grey seal comes to the surface to eat larger fish which are held in the mouth and torn into smaller, more easily swallowed pieces with the claws on the front flippers.

DAY 13b

I'm tired again after all that play with mum in the bay. I'm having a good stretch and a yawn before having a well-earned sleep on the beach.

Amazing Factfile

Although typically diving to depths of between 30 to 70 metres when feeding, grey seals have been known to dive to depths of around 300 metres.

DAY 14a

Like all pups, I love to play.   Here, I have found a bit of kelp in the shallow waters.

Amazing Factfile

Seals have twice the amount of blood that is found in terrestrial animals of similar size. On deeper dives they can slow their heart rate down to fewer than 20 beats per minute in order to conserve oxygen.

DAY 14b

It's time for a feed and, because I love the water so much, mum is now tending to feed me at the water's edge rather than on the beach.

Amazing Factfile

Grey seals will dive for around eight minutes when foraging for food, but while at rest or at sleep, they may remain submerged for up to 20 minutes.

49

DAY 15a

It's just bliss to be able to float and relax in the water with mum.

Amazing Factfile

The grey seal can swim at speeds of 20 knots (around 23 miles per hour) when it is pursuing its prey, although most of the time it cruises at about two or three knots.

DAY 15b

Sometimes when we're playing, I can become a little over-excited and have a little nibble at mum's neck. As she has a thick layer of blubber around her neck, it probably doesn't hurt but she doesn't seem to mind in any case.

Amazing Factfile

In areas of good visibility, the grey seal hunts by sight alone. The large eyes are especially adapted to see underwater with the lens structured to allow as much light in as possible. When on land, the eyes are protected from bright sunlight by closing the pupil.

DAY 16

After another play session, I am resting up cheek-to-cheek with mum amongst the rocks on the water's edge.

Amazing Factfile

In deeper waters, where light levels are poorer, the seal depends primarily on its highly sensitive underwater directional hearing. Even a blind grey seal has no problem catching prey. The ears cannot be seen because there are no external ear flaps.

DAY 17a

I've been playing amongst the rocks today and a piece of seaweed has been caught on my face.

Amazing Factfile

The grey seal also hunts by using its sensitive whiskers, called 'vibrissae', that grow on either side of its snout and above the eyes, which detect movement vibration.

DAY 17b

It's quite nice just to lie relaxed in the water. I think that one of my most endearing features are my large, dark eyes.

Amazing Factfile

> *While hunting, the grey seal emits a series of clicking sounds which may have a function in the echolocation of prey similar to that used by dolphin species.*

DAY 18

Sound asleep with eyes tightly closed, the sensitive whiskers around my nose and eyes can be seen clearly.

Amazing Factfile

It is also possible that the grey seal can follow fish by sensing changes in the chemical composition of the water.

DAY 19a

Although I cried for mum yesterday, she didn't come to me. I am no longer being fed and she has left me completely to look after myself from now on and I will not see her again. We have had lots of opportunities to bond, especially when playing in the water and she has been a very attentive mother who has fed me regularly on her fat-rich milk for the past 18 days.

I now weigh between 45 and 50 kilogrammes - over three times my birth weight. I will live off my fat reserves until I enter the water independently and I am able to feed for myself.

Amazing Factfile

In the seal world, there's no such thing as being too fat! In the cold waters of the North Sea, grey seals have 6 centimetres of blubber to keep them warm. Their cylindrical shape not only makes them streamlined for swimming, but minimises heat loss too.

DAY 19b

Now that mum has left me, she is ready to mate with the grey seal bull that has been patrolling the bay. Although they are mating in the shallow waters, this bull has mated with other mothers on the beach as well.

Amazing Factfile

Having mated, implantation is delayed for around two and a half months, followed by a gestation period of around 9 months, so that the cow is ready to give birth about the same time, on the same beach, the following year.

DAY 20

I have found an old inner tube from a tractor tyre which has been washed up on to the beach. I am using this as a comfort blanket in the absence of mum.

Amazing Factfile

During the time that the mother is feeding her pup, she rarely feeds, losing up to a quarter of her body weight before her pup is weaned. In order to build up the necessary fat reserves to prepare for this period of fasting, as well as to prepare for her future developing foetus, the female grey seal actively feeds during the months prior to the breeding season.

DAY 21a

I have now started to moult and it's really quite itchy! You can see some of the fur from my head where I have been rubbing against the old inner tube.

Amazing Factfile

The males also actively feed during the months prior to the breeding season because they will fast for the six weeks or so of the breeding season where they will fight off other bulls in order to mate with as many cows as possible.

DAY 21b

Even my flippers have started to moult!

Amazing Factfile

Grey seals are from the group of animals called pinnipeds meaning 'winged feet', referring to their flippers, which are especially adapted for life at sea. The long, sturdy claws on the front flippers of the grey seal help it to move on land, particularly when it needs to grip onto rocks or ice.

DAY 22

I'm not looking at my best when I am moulting. I'm definitely having a bad hair day today!

Amazing Factfile

When a seal swims quickly, it holds its front flippers tightly against its sides, and propels itself with its powerful hind flippers. When the seal is swimming slowly, the front flippers are used as stabilisers and stick out to the sides.

DAY 23

I'm not using a favourite rock as a scratching post like most of the other pups who are moulting and I have left the area that I was using around the old inner tube. Instead, I've decided just to move around and explore the beach. You can see that my juvenile fur is now quite clear on my head and flippers.

Amazing Factfile

Most mammals need to maintain a body temperature of 37⁰C. Whilst the grey seal's layer of blubber protects against the cold seas, it is such a good insulator that, when hauled out, it may sometimes overheat. The grey seal's flippers have a large peripheral blood supply that allows the heat to escape and it cools itself down by waving its flippers in the air.

DAY 24a

As well as moulting on my head and flippers, I have now started to moult on my chest, tummy and tail. My white fur has been rubbed away because I've been moving around the beach so much. My smooth, adult, patterned fur is much more obvious now and I look as if I'm wearing a white, furry jacket.

Amazing Factfile

The grey seal has much shorter limbs than most mammals: what appear to be the armpit and groin of the seal are, in fact, the wrist and ankle. By comparison, the bones on their flippers are enormously long, and the skin between them forms a web which is used like a paddle to propel the seal along.

DAY 24b

Despite the fact that I'm in the middle of moulting, the draw of the water is just too tempting and I've decided to go back into the bay for a swim today. It feels strange not to have mum to play with. However, unlike my white fur, my juvenile fur is waterproof so I should be more mobile and agile in the water from now on.

Amazing Factfile

> *Immediately after the breeding season, both male and female grey seals have a period of feeding when they regain condition. After that, during the spring, hormone changes prompt them to undergo their annual moult when they spend long periods hauled out, though not at the breeding sites.*

DAY 25a

I'm resting back at my inner tube today as the snow begins to fall. However, I do not feel the cold because of the insulation from my thick layer of blubber.

Amazing Factfile

Juvenile seals usually moult first, followed by females and finally by adult males, although there is overlap in the coming and going. The moult might take as long as six weeks to complete, during which time the seals are often irritable and listless. Once their new hair has grown, the grey seals head out to sea to resume feeding.

DAY 25b

It's snowing a bit more heavily as I play around the water's edge. My white fur really is becoming quite patchy now.

Amazing Factfile

These haul-out sites can be large - sometimes forming groups of several hundred animals - and very noisy. Grey seals are vocal with a wide range of social calls when hauled out on land ranging from growls, snarls, hisses and barking, while at sea they will communicate with a series of grunts, clicks and roars.

DAY 26

As I rest up on the beach today, I'm almost there as far as the moulting goes with just a few tufts of puppy fur here and there. I'm beginning to look more like a juvenile grey seal rather than a pup. As my fur is black with lighter blotches, you can now tell that I am a male.

Amazing Factfile

Grey seals spend about two-thirds of their time at sea but will come ashore to breed, to moult and to rest between fishing expeditions where they can be seen hauled out on rocks and islands not far from the shore, looking like great grey bananas in the sun.

DAY 27

It's another big day today in my amazing adventure. Today is the day that I am fully moulted and I look like a juvenile grey seal rather than a pup. I'm going to rest up on the beach all day because I have a big day ahead of me tomorrow. Here, I'm using a rock as a pillow to rest my head.

Amazing Factfile

Humans have had a long relationship with grey seals. They have proved to be amenable to life in captivity and were commonly found in zoos around their native range, particularly Europe. Traditionally, grey seals were popular circus animals and often used in performances such as balancing and display acts.

DAY 28a

This is the final day of my amazing adventure. Sometimes pups continue to stay on at the rookery for a week or two after they are fully moulted and rest up before heading off to sea, but I'm not hanging around. I've headed off down to the bay in my fully waterproof juvenile grey seal fur.

However, rather than head straight out to sea, I'm going to play amongst the rocks to get myself prepared. The bay is quite calm today so it is a good day to start the next stage of my amazing adventure.

When I do head out into the North Sea, I will have to learn to feed for myself. If this takes me a little time, I will live off my reserves of blubber until I can fish efficiently.

Amazing Factfile

Humans have hunted the grey seal for thousands of years. Its skin was used to make clothing and its blubber made into oil used in lamps, as medication and for softening leather. In some areas, its flesh was also eaten.

DAY 28b

And so, as I wave farewell to my beach, I am now ready to head off into the North Sea where I may wander over a wide distance, perhaps even over 1,000 kilometres.

If I travel south, I may go to the Isle of May in the Firth of Forth or, further south still, to the Farne Islands off the Northumberland coast. If I head north, I may end up at the Orkney Islands or, even further north, I may arrive at the Shetland Islands. If I go due east, I may find other grey seal colonies along the Norwegian coastline.

Whatever direction I travel, I am sure that I will continue with my amazing adventure.

Amazing Factfile

In 1914, the UK grey seal population was thought to number only 500, and subsequently grey seals were the first mammals to be protected by modern legislation – the Grey Seals Protection Act of 1914. Today, the Conservation of Seals Act (1970), (replaced in Scotland by the Marine (Scotland) Act 2010), protects grey seals during a closed season from 1ˢᵗ September to 31ˢᵗ December, although seals causing damage to fishing nets can still be killed legally.

References

The following websites were used as reference:

Conserve Ireland   www.conserveireland.com

Cornish Seal Sanctuary   www.sealsanctuary.co.uk

Encyclopaedia of Earth   www.eoearth.org

Hebridean Whale and Dolphin Trust   www.whaledolphintrust.co.uk

Scottish Natural Heritage   www.snh.org.uk

The Mammal Society   www.mammal.org.uk

Wild Scotland   www.wild-scotland.org.uk

Nature in Shetland   www.nature-shetland.co.uk